NOT FADE AWAY

Also available by Adrian Henri

Collected Poems (Allison & Busby, 1986)
Wish You Were Here (Cape, 1990)
The Wakefield Mysteries (Methuen, 1991)

ADRIAN HENRI
Not Fade Away
•POEMS 1989-1994•

BLOODAXE BOOKS

ISBN: 1 85224 313 9

First published 1994 by
Bloodaxe Books Ltd,
P.O. Box 1SN,
Newcastle upon Tyne NE99 1SN.

Bloodaxe Books Ltd acknowledges
the financial assistance of Northern Arts.

Cover printing by J. Thomson Colour Printers Ltd, Glasgow.

Printed in Great Britain by
Cromwell Press Ltd, Broughton Gifford, Melksham, Wiltshire.

For Catherine,
in whatever country we are

Acknowledgements

Acknowledgements are due to the editors of the following publications in which some of these poems first appeared: *Ambit, Art Quarterly, Artspool, Box* (Mammoth/Teens), *Fatchance, The Green Book, Klaonica: poems for Bosnia* (Bloodaxe Books/*The Independent*, 1993), *Poetry Review* and *Spokes*.

'Winter Ending' was published in the Labour Party's election manifesto in April 1992. 'Annus Mirabilis' was written for BBC Radio 3's *Table Talk*. 'André Breton at Varengeville', 'La Mer' and 'Souvenirs' were written for *Souvenirs of Normandy*, with music by Andy Roberts, for the Brighton Festival, 1992.

The cover painting, *The Entry of Christ into Liverpool* by Adrian Henri, is from the collection of Bob Simm.

Contents

LOOK, STRANGER...

A PORTRAIT OF THE ARTIST

A Portrait of the Artist
(in memoriam Sam Walsh)

In a forgotten attic smelling faintly of soot
propped against a peeling wall,
there is a painting,
wrapped in a moth-eaten tartan rug.
Next to it, linked by cobwebs, flakes of plaster,
the mummified bodies of spiders,
there is a battered, dark red portfolio
with black, triangular corners,
the black tapes that used to fasten it missing.
In it the artist kept his dreams.

There is a dream
of painting a giant replica of the Pier Head
to be installed at Woodside Ferry;
of one-man shows held weekly
on the pavement at Cazeneau Street market;
of a portrait of Ingrid Bergman
her haloed, backlit hair
painted as tenderly as Alfred Hitchcock,
the shadow across her cheekbone
painted as delicately as Michael Curtiz;
of himself playing the John Wayne part
in a remake of *The Quiet Man:*
there is a final dream
the artist did not dream,
of paintings of Saddam Hussain
and General Norman Schwarzkopf,
huge as war memorials.

Beneath the rug
there is a painting.
It is a portrait of the artist,
unfinished.
The artist, black beard trimmed neatly,
high cheekbones, dark hair falling
across his forehead,
looks out of the picture
which he has forgotten.

Behind him the model lies,
waiting patiently,
her shell-pink body
painted in the manner of Lucas Cranach.
A wisp of spray-paint
seems to indicate a room
not unlike this attic.

The artist gazes out at us;
carefully painted highlights catch
the glimpse of mockery in his eyes.
He does not see the gleaming, skeleton hand,
painted in the manner of Hans Holbein,
place an opened bottle of whisky
silently on a table by the easel.

The dust in the attic stirs for a moment,
then settles; a few tiny motes
catch the late afternoon sunlight.

Camille Claudel

Someone has stolen her God.

Her smoothest flanks untouched.

She sleeps like a doll
on the dunes above the shoreline:
the cruel birds,
under guise of nesting,
gather, gather.

Clair de Lune
(for Laurie Lee)

The poet
points his white stick
at the moon.
'Is it full?'
he asks.

Honeysuckle, Butterfly, Rose

And her far seas moan as a single shell,
And her grove glow with love-lit fires of Troy
D.G. ROSSETTI, 'Venus'

Golden aureole, palest areola
more delicate than roses,
hair haloed with brimstone butterflies

Honeysuckle, butterfly, rose,
apple and dart

Heart cleansed of all
but the sight of white breasts,
prouder than envious flowers

Apple and dart,
honeysuckle, butterfly, rose

Coarse stamens strain
for that dark grove where far seas moan,
as in a single shell

Honeysuckle, butterfly, rose,
apple and dart

Pierced by her eyes wherein no glimpse
of love-lit fires, sudden as marigolds
found in a winter castle

Apple and dart,
honeysuckle, butterfly, rose

Virgin and Magdalen,
apple and dart,
Eve, Lady Lilith;
only to taste the forbidden secrets,

Honeysuckle, butterfly,
butterfly, rose.

(after D.G. Rossetti: 'Venus Verticordia')

The White Ball

(after Ivan Puni: 'Construction With White Ball', 1915)

'What is this?'
the eager museum lady asks;
'A Ball!' 'A Ball!'
chorus the children.
She tosses them words –
'synthesis', 'construction',
'colour' –
they wait in vain
to catch a white ball.

The Triumph of the Innocents

(after William Holman Hunt)

'The Triumph of the Innocents':
how weary that inner sense
of triumph, despite the leering faces
amongst the crowd, the whispered voices
in the night, the fight to paint
each chubby thigh, each rainbow bubble,
to get it right, despite the siren songs,
the alien smells, the endless trouble.
Why did the canvas split just there?
Sometimes I feel not even my best friends
care, cannot see my plight. To make
each infant real and yet ethereal
as moonlight. Even more difficult
to fight this lonely fight with him;
Jacob's with the Angel no worse than mine.

Once more to the mastic and the turpentine...

André Breton at Varengeville

In the round tower where doves dream
her name is the beginning of hope. Unable
to forget the moment in the Rue Lafayette,
chance encounters haunted
as the man who constantly meets himself
in the cinema. Her eyes the colour of fernleaves,
filled with echoes of regret
that hang in the cast-iron roofs
of railway stations, eyes that speak
of city streets
VINS   BOIS   CHARBONS
of the magic of dark passageways,
tantalising as cream silken promises,
the statue in the suburban park at dusk.

'L'Étreinte de la Pieuvre':
In the darkened picture-palace of your dreams
it seems that only the fearless poet
(and his intrepid helper Sandy McNab)
can rescue the lovely Ruth
from the octopus tentacles, the satanic gaze
of the fiendish Doctor Wang Poo.

Sloping evening light from the West
fills the hollow between her breasts
where the steep path leads to the sea;
last lingering trace
of that delicate smell,
the taste of rockpool, seashell,
the pink embrace of sea-anemones,
carried on the wind.

Her name is the beginning of hope,
but only the beginning.

Now,
I watch her lying in the sun,
like a cat watching a butterfly.

La Mer

Claude Debussy at Pourville

Footsteps in the snow
across the white page
the sudden swell
of bells beneath the sea
cathedrale engloutie
white notes glide
like sails
across the darkened harbour.

Siren-song of your eyes
green stream
that drags me down unseen
Ondine
seaweed parts   reveals your smile
brown arms embrace
drowned   last memory
of your face
feux d'artifice
fade against night waters.

Blue for Slim

(in memoriam Slim Galliard)

Cement mixer don't putty-putty no more
Cement mixer don't putty-putty no more
Cos my man Slim has gone to Lethe's shore

There's silence down on 52nd Street
Silence all down 52nd Street
Couldn't hear the King of Vouti's beat

Went to Laguna, watched the tide come in
Went to Laguna, watched the tide come in
Searched the beach but couldn't see my Slim

No I'm dunkin' bagels back in Liverpool town
Dunkin' bagels back in Liverpool town
Thinking of Slim as the Mersey sun goes down

Cement mixer don't go putty-putty no more
Cement mixer don't go putty-putty no more
Cos my man Slim has gone to Lethe's shore

A Brief Reflection on Poetry

(for Miroslav Holub)

The poem
reflects briefly on itself.
The blackboard
behind it
in the Music Room
briefly reflects it:
breve, semibreve,
quaver, semiquaver;
in the silence after the poem
the ghost of a violin
quavers briefly.

Venus Rising

(after Guercino: 'A Woman Seated on a Bed Raising a Curtain')

Woman or goddess?
Tawny shadows
caress your belly
like strokes of a pen;
once again,
night's curtain drawn back,
hair tousled in the light.
Venus or woman,
your remembered smell
still haunts the morning bedclothes.

Regatta
(after James Tissot)

To touch the warmth
beneath the striped bustle,
lost in your eyes
behind the veil.
Your hand surreptitious
on my blazered sleeve.
Thoughts, desires
tangled as the rigging behind us.
Phantom kisses in river sunlight.

(for Juliet)

Memphis Sunset

You forgot to remember to forget
how the sun came up at 78 r.p.m.
a battered panel truck
parked in the studio back lot
until the blue moon set over Kentucky.

All around the world
every boy and girl heard the news
there was good rockin' in Memphis
put on their rockin' shoes.

But this time they made you a mountain,
a mountain you really couldn't climb.
Impossible. Its rhinestone slopes,
Lone Star peaks, impassable.
Impassive avalanches of applause,
snowblind in the spotlights.

An echoing voice
says you have now left the stadium,
scuffed blue suede shoes
forgotten in the dressing room.

Outside,
the black stretch limo waits.

SOUVENIRS

Souvenirs

(for John and Anne Willett)

Chocolate sardines, torn election-posters MAR
CHAIS, huddled sheep before a distant sepia
view of Pourville. The yellow-and-grey world
of Lords and Ladies on the wallpaper in
the *lingerie*. Lemon light. Night hydrangeas.
The smell of the ferry, scrubbed mussels
deep blue in a white bowl in the electric kitchen,
where moths beat against the windowpane. Blinding
rain that wipes away the cliffs at Etretat.

Green depths of evening *sous-bois*, tall trees
that shutter the light along the banks outside
the villages. A black workman's suit, a sailor's cap
bought beside St Jacques. *Oeufs de Pâques.*
Andouillettes, and mackerel cooked with driftwood
on the beach. Each stone that I've brought home
since 1968. Late light across the harvestfields
from Ambrumesnil. Cattle dream, creamy as caramel.
The smell across the valley from the Nescafé factory.

The tall gingko tree that split ten years ago,
one twin trunk that still lies overgrown,
immutable as memory.

Death Valley

Yea, though I drive
airconditioned
through the Valley of the Shadow
of Death,
still I fear
its ancient evil;
the unblinking rocks,
the unforgiving heat:
Nissan and Misubishi
do not comfort me.

Garden, Barlaston

Rich leather leaves of whitebeam
scattered white side up,
evergreen sheen of rhododendron,
turned hopefully to the November sun:
the willowherb's white cursive
writes summer's testament
against sleek holly,
dying privet.

Fallen Appletree, Normandy

It lies on the grass,
winded,
orange and yellow fruit
hung like Christmas lights
in the bare, brown,
summer branches.

We take a photograph.

The image develops,
slowly,
in winter darkness.

Impressions d'Afrique

I *Chaloupe*

The deck
of the ferry to Gorée
lurches away
from my waiting feet
like the words
I want to say;
images that avoid me,
bright, flamboyant
as a poinciana tree,
the light
on the still-misted sea.

II *Conference*

We talk of tradition,
putting new wine
in old bottles.
For Hawad
the poem is the marks
left by tent-pegs
when the camp has moved on.
For Zinsou
the poet must leave
to find new words
alone in the forest.
Behind us,
they are unloading
boxes of new wine
in old bottles.

III *Departure*

Last day on Gorée
the sun comes out to say
'*Bonjour, ça va?*'
and stays, persistent as
the vendors who won't go away,
loud as the playground-sound
of kids that splash in the bay.

IV *A Poem Instead of a Postcard*

Dear Janine,
                    A postcard from the edge
of Africa. *Impressions d'Afrique.*
Only a week, and already memories
come and go, regular as the ferry,
regular as thoughts of her, despite
the catwalk grace of girls on the beach,
each with an invisible load on her head;
skin so black that it refracts the light,
as evening sprawls across the harbour,
staining dark red walls a darker red.
I sit on the terrace for hours. The fish
is delicious. Can't wait to paint
the flowers. I want to stay.
                                   love,
                                   A.

The Parsonage, Haworth

In the earth, the earth thou shalt be laid,
A grey stone standing over thee;
Black mould beneath thee spread,
And black mould to cover thee.
EMILY BRONTË

Gravestones piled deep as fallen leaves,
trodden into the sodden ground;
last consumptive flush of Autumn
in the sycamores;
a kissing-gate swings disused
in the bitter wind.

Cries of crows, rattle of rain,
on the nursery windowpane;
insistent tick of the grandfather clock,
insistent tock of the stonemason's hammer,
stammered epitaphs
swathed in lichened green.

It is not the stone that eats their bodies,
but the black spring that runs through them
that feeds the dark sarcophagus.

A glimpse of sun
sudden as a blush suffusing soft cheeks;
pale blue eyes
calling through blonde coppices of hair
across the dimpled moors.

Giverny Revisited

(for Pamela Bradshaw)

Revisited by you, too,
though I didn't know. Knew
only through poems read in summer,
of Claude in the garden,
Alice indoors, the voices of children
as he, and we, planted words
in springtime, dreaming
of summer gardens.

Wye

I sit by the river
with notebook and pen
while thoughts, like swans,
glide away again:
'Oh', she says,
stopping to look,
'I'd like to take a leaf
out of his book.'

Oudewater

(for Irene)

In this town of witches
where they were weighed
and sometimes found wanting,
I think of the witchcraft
of shadowed dimples,
eyes that change like the sea;
I weigh these words you will not hear
and find them wanting.

*Oudewater is a small town in Holland where suspected witches were weighed in a
public weigh house: if they weighed less than the average for their height they were
presumed to have sold their souls to the devil and found guilty.*

From an Antique Land

1

Cows browse
in the Basilica
black-and-white
against black columns.

Eyes blue
in the basalt darkness
glow like poppies.

Umm Quais.

2

She waits patient at the gate
for us, tattooed patterns
on her face, weathered
as the desert.
          The child
who clings to her black skirts
wears a Mickey Mouse T-shirt.

Quasr Hamam al Sarak.

3

Schoolgirls in long blue dresses,
whitescarved heads,
blossom in the lunchtime street
like bougainvillaea.

Amman.

4

A chameleon
ignores the laws
of Justinian
on a granite wall.

Quasr el Hallorat.

5

Mirages shimmer
false mirages of polythene
shimmer too.

Umm el Rasas – Kerak.

6 Bedouin

He picks his way
along the track
carefully
not separating
the sheep
from the goats.

7 Petra

Pink palaces
beyond the dreams of postmen,
rose-red rocks
beyond the dreams of palettes,
wait to be reborn
beyond the dark passage.

8

I smear my mouth with Vaseline
my lips dry
for lack of your kisses.

(for Catherine)

9

The Caliph sits in majesty
above the dancing-girls, the graffiti;
the painted Zodiac awaits
Eid, and the rising of the moon,
a sugared almond in the sky.

Quasr Amara / Petra.

10 *Aphrodite*

She dances
– tiny, golden,
voluptuous –
to unheard music
in a museum case
in Liverpool.

Jordan / Liverpool
April – October 1991

YOSEMITE

Yosemite

You are my Yosemite
all your deep declivities
– Schwarzwald, Colden Valley,
Col de Rousset –
and you are my Pacific
– the taste of sealrock and surf,
pinemist and clamshell –
the rounded slopes of childhood
– Moel Fammau, Moel Maen Eva –
chapels riding their sides
in the Sion morning:
the blue remembered hills
– Wenlock Edge, Long Mynd,
The Wrekin –
that heave their forest fleece
into bedroom daylight.

Café

Under the auspices of night
a louring sky
and the ominous waiter
I watch you
dancing in your head.

When you look at me like that
I feel like a television set
waiting for you to turn me off.

The Cerise Swimsuit

(after William Carlos Williams)

so much depends
upon

a cerise swim
suit

hung out to
dry

in Laurel
Canyon

Thanksgiving

A storm,
its fur rubbed up the wrong way,
lowers over the heart of England,
like the memory of harsh words
waiting for the DON'T WALK sign.

The sun,
battling like Turner through the waves,
lifts the heart, the horizon,
like the warmth of a kiss
at the subway turnstile.

Some Other Guy

'Trick or treat'
behind the mask
I lurk in your street
hoping for kisses.

'A penny for the guy'
outside your gate
I lie, disguised,
wait for a smile.

You warm your hands
at someone else's bonfire;
rockets, Catherine-wheels explode
in someone else's garden.

Thicket

Like
the childhood undergrowth
of woods
shrunk now
to an average-sized coppice,
the thrill
still lurks within;
the fear,
green darkness
smelling of elderberry and
blackberry leaves:
the urge to push
beyond the bright pith
of snapped twigs
to the dark heart within,
warm, amniotic;
smell faint and distinct
as memory.

Snowman

After I'd made a snowman
I used to cry with the pain;
not out in the cold, but by the fire
when my hands were warm again.

It's freezing here today;
sometimes it's just the same:
it's when we're warm together
I suddenly feel the pain.

Reassurance

'...Well, the boot is on the other foot now.'

'Yes, the boot is on the other foot now,
and I'm limping.'

Harvest Festival

Your new knickers
are patterned with fruit;
redcurrant and blackcurrant,
apple and blackberry,
ripe gooseberries,
tumble against black:
I bury my face
in their abundance,
the rich smell of autumn.
All good gifts around us...

We plough the fields and scatter

All safely gathered in,
we celebrate the harvest;
dark green leaves, orange-red fruit,
yellow flowers.

Thunderstorm, Nice

Lemons glow in the half-light;
Adam and Eve in the first rainstorm,
we hear the thunder,
see the shells of tortoises shine
like grapes washed on the vine;
the final tremors flicker between us,
last drops of rain on the oleander.

Rock Climber, Avon Gorge

I stand by your side
like Robert the Bruce
and watch him,
redtrousered,
try, try, try again
to scale the indifferent strata,
twinges of vertigo
through the soles of my feet
at the chasm
suspended
between us.

Oxford, Sunday, Rain

Sunday. Wet quadrangles,
the harsh angles of Gothic towers,
indifferent cobbles underfoot.
It is always like this, rain,
the bus from The High, sometimes
a taxi, this time the last time.
A face at the latticed window,
Bodleian treasuries of memories.
Backpacked tourists huddle
in their anoraks. The train at Platform 2
is ten minutes late. It is always like this.
Sunday. Rain. The remembered taste.
A train. Dreaming choirs of birds
sing evensong in the evening garden
behind your room. 'I'll ring when I get back.
See you soon.' The train lurches late
through the growing gloom.

Winter Garden

There is a garden in her face
Where roses and white lilies grow

The bathwater smelling of blackberries,
my hair of white nettles, my body
soaped with the scent of green ferns.

We walked in the Botanical Gardens
in winter. Small pink flowers
against the gloom. Berries bloomed,
cherry ripe. You rang, this morning.
There is a garden in this place,
of sorts. A lone honeysuckle
huddles against the frost, that rimes
the unchecked weeds of summer,
brown stalks of lily-of-the-valley.

O ruddier than the cherry,
O brighter than the berry

Tonight I meet you from the plane.
All I can offer, once again,
a winter garden,
the smell of blackberries, green ferns,
white nettles.

LOOK, STRANGER...

Look, Stranger...

Look, stranger, at this island now...
W.H. AUDEN

End of the Road

Between *The Way We Were*
and *The Pine Centre* we pine
for the past, thrill to sandblasted,
ex-Satanic mills reflected
in the still canal. Is it you there,
weeping behind the Muzak
in The Orwell Pub,
Eric Blair?

Wigan, 1990

Young Man On a Train, May 1st, 1990

Indolent,
he shields his eyes from the sun
with *Thus Spake Zarathustra*;
his personal stereo, gone public,
pollutes the air like cigarette-smoke:
he does not see the blazing candlewick
of rapefields, the punctual mayblossom,
the bright lodges.

Two Pastorales

1

Fat blue foreman in hard white hat,
why do you walk through the fields like that,
missing so much and so much?

2

A peterade of tractors:
beside the lake, beneath the trees,
spluttering and farting in the breeze.

Nocturne: Rhyl Sands
(for David Cox and Martin O'Connor)

tights
and sand
sights
of land
and water
beyond the lights
on summer nights

beneath
the pier
a pair
of crumpled tights
mute evidence
of love's delights

Back Gardens

That morning regret
yet again;
seeing from a train
patios and greenhouses,
bright plastic toys,
carousels of washing,
satellite-discs and rockeries,
louvred garage doors:
nostalgia for a vanished world
I never knew.

Fin de Vacances

The holidays are over:
polythene containers safely stowed
in the red plastic zip-topped bag;
the final rains unrained,
the final phone-numbers exchanged,
the unmeant 'see-you-next-year's said
the colourslides, the Super 8s, the videotapes
already projected on unremembering walls;
the luggage waits accusing in the hall,
the note put out for the milkman,
the neighbours thanked for minding the cat,
straw hats pushed to the back of wardrobes,
souvenirs all ready, waiting to be sent.
Now, something nice out of a tin, and telly,
and start again.

Poet in School

'Write about
something that's happened to you
or someone you know.' Half an hour
to go, and still nothing written.
Just sitting, face blank as the empty sheet,
shuffling his feet. 'Come on, son,
you must know something that's happened
to someone.' 'No, Sir.'
'Your family, your friends?'
'Sir, my brother's best mate died.'
'How?' 'Sir, electrocuted. A train...'
'Was he on the track?' 'Sir...'
The empty eyes fill with tears.
Somehow the years between us
aren't enough to take the words back.

Buckinghamshire ARTS

_____ **A** SSOCIATION _____

55 High Street, Aylesbury, Bucks HP20 1SA
Aylesbury (0296) 434704

BOOK THE WRITER

CLAIM FOR REIMBURSEMENT

<u>REPORT BY ORGANISER</u> (which must be completed before subsidy is released)

Please comment on the visit made by the writer named overleaf, with reference
to the format of the visit, audience response, arrangements, and whether you
would wish to invite this writer again. Details of any variation which had to
be made to the visit should also be noted.

Name of Writer: Adrian Henri

Date of Visit:

Establishment: Little Kingshill Co. Co.
                                           School
Age-Range of Audience:
                              11+ & 12+

Number Attending:
                          60
Signed: *Frances Massey* Date: 8/5/87

Mr. Adrian Henri was punctual.

His talk was lively, imaginative and informative - enjoyed by
both adults and children.

Unfortunately his personal appearance left much to be desired and
did nothing to reinforce the standards of dress and hygiene held within
the school.

It also did nothing to improve the image of Liverpool, a city in
need of ambassadors.

50

What Jossie Said

Jossie said
their dog ate their cat:
it did, just like that
– so Jossie said –
one minute it was purring,
the next it was dead
– so Jossie said –
he did, right out in class;
it ate it all except the head
– so Jossie said –
it left *that* on his Mother's bed,
just like *The Godfather*
– so Jossie said –
a little black head
tangled up in the sheet
right by her feet
– so Jossie said –
they say
you could hear her two doors away.

Well,
that's what Jossie said.

Spare the Face

refusing the blindfold
I watch you make the expected
daily
phonecall to him
head held high
gazing bravely into the gunbarrels.

The Life of Riley

1

Riley
was born with a silver spoon
in his mouth.
'Riley'
said his Mother
'take that silver spoon
out of your mouth
and stir yourself.'

2

Riley's
Nanny and
Riley's
Granny
spoilt him something rotten,
blessed his little cotton
socks each Sunday,
put them in the wash
on Monday.

3

When he was three
they cut down the laurel trees.
Riley
danced and sang
and went round selling logs
to the neighbours.

4

Clever
Riley
was top of the class,
ace at English, best at Maths;
handsome
Riley
set hearts a-flutter,
went through the Sixth Form
like a knife through butter.

5

Riley
decided to go into the City,
fought like a tiger,
showed no pity;
bought them long
and sold them short,
went for broke,
never got caught.

6

Rapidly promoted
from Lieutenant,
Riley
became a Captain of Industry,
only keeping company
with Company cars,
smoking cigars,
drinking champagne
in expensive bars
(on account
of his expense account).

7

A beggar advances
with outstretched hand
'I'm beggared if I will'
said
Riley
not giving him the time of day.

8

'Every cloud
has a silver lining'
said
Riley,
riding in his Silver Cloud,
busy
lining his pockets.

9

Riley
had a model house
and a model life,
2.5 children and an ex-
model wife,
who he later changed
for a this year's model.

10

Riley
grew old dis-
gracefully. Jetsetter
with a bus pass.
International playboy,
pensioner toyboy.

11

In his declining years
Riley
declined to be interviewed
about his charmed lives
and charming wives
(not to mention
shadier ladies)
disclosed all
full-and-frankly
in his Autobiography
for an undisclosed fee.

12

'I've lived the life of
Riley'
thought
Riley,
carefully rehearsing
his Famous Last Words.

Dancing through the Dark

It's Friday night and you can live your dreams
It's Friday night and in the lights it seems
There's no one else but you
Dancing through the dark

It's Friday night and you've just washed your hair
It's Friday night and no one seems to care
What Saturday will say
Dancing through the dark

It's Friday night, your Giro's nearly gone
It's Friday night, and you're the only one
The music's playing for
Dancing through the dark

It's Friday night, the Disco lights are bright,
You've found the one for you, a dream come true,
Until the lights go out at two
Dancing through the dark
Dancing
Dancing through the dark

Annus Mirabilis

Gourmet eating began
In nineteen sixty-three
(Which was much too soon for me) –
Between the end of the *Chatterley* ban
And the Beatles' first LP.

The nearest thing was a Somali café
called *The Verlyn*, to begin with;
soon to change to *The Silver Moon*.
Meat curry half-a-crown,
the cheapest meal in town:
and sixpence more for chicken,
as a treat. We'd eat there
on Saturdays, before the pub.
Grub at home was Paprika Chicken,
made by Joyce, when times were good;
not much choice, when they weren't:
Spag. Bol., spare ribs, scouse, maybe
liver, onions and gravy. And
always chips from Harry's on the way home.

So eating was never better than
In nineteen sixty-three
(Though a little early for me) –
Between the end of the *Chatterley* ban
And the Beatles' first LP.

Party

Sitting on the stairs,
you tell me that when you were five
a boy called David Bird tried to kiss you,
missed, and fell into a bed of nettles.

I want to kiss you now,
but what would I fall off,
and what would I fall into?

Too late I move, indecisively,
and fall into the nettles.

Someone takes you gently by the hand,
smooths your hair,
leads you back into the party.

Jessica

I wish I was fifteen again. I mean
she's lovely, Jessica, I wouldn't be without her
for the world. I don't remember the pain,
just her curled up bright red in the hospital cot,
and me with Mars bars and Jackie Collins. I suppose
I've missed a lot; I'm eighteen but I'm really sixteen,
I've somehow lost the two years in between.
My Mum and Dad have been great, and the teachers, too:
sometimes I'm late and they're OK, even if
I have to stay away. Anyway, I'm doing 'A' levels now.
English, French and Art. I remember when
the contractions started I was watching *Neighbours*:
sixteen hours later I was still in labour.
But she's worth every minute, Jessica.
Claire's seven months gone and it doesn't show.
She doesn't seem to care: only a few mates know,
she hasn't told her Mum or anyone. I think
she thinks it will just go away.
                              What was I going to say?
Oh, yes. The worst day was when I got done for shoplifting.
We only did it for fun. Five hours in a police cell.
I used to tell them I was staying with friends.
Didn't do much, really: stayed on the station all night once,
drinking cheap wine. Now it's fine, I've got
more than enough to do, with Jessica. It's funny,
having to think for two. It was so *boring*
being thirteen, nothing to do round here
but get into trouble, know what I mean?
Him? I haven't seen him in years,
and I don't particularly want to.
We don't need a man. Homework gives me
something to think about besides Cow and Gate
and Napisan. Anyway, I'll have to go, I'll be late.
I don't want to make her wait: they've gone for a walk.
I think she means as much to her as she does to me,
Jessica. It's true. Dad too. Soon she'll be three.
College for me, if I get good grades.

The doctors and nurses all called me *Mrs*,
as if I was someone's wife. Strange,
how one night and a few kisses
can change your life.

Uncle Bill

Uncle Bill would roll home once a week
watched by the Birkenhead moon, along
the railings of the Park. Soon, a few people
would wait in the dark until he rolled uphill
and into view. It's true: every Friday night,
regular as clockwork. Even the traffic-lights
used to wait up for him.

Uncle Bill, Uncle Bill,
Rolling, rolling up the hill
in Tranmere.

Uncle Bill hadn't got a swallow,
my Mother used to say. Dad said
his legs were hollow. He'd roll to bed,
all the way up the stairs, too. Once
he trod on the cat, and rolled
all the way down again. 'Men,' Gran said,
helping him to his feet.

Uncle Bill, Uncle Bill,
Rolling, rolling up the hill
in Sydney Road.

Uncle Bill would stay all night in *The Crooked Billet*,
empty his pint, hand it to the barmaid to fill it,
then down the next in one. Gone. He'd wait a week
for the next Friday night treat. Then home again,
along the railings, full from his boots
to his shiny head. Dead now, no more smell
of corduroy and horses.

Uncle Bill, Uncle Bill,
Probably still drinks his Friday fill,
Rolling back along the clouds somewhere.

Uncle Bill, Uncle Bill,
Rolling home, rolling home.

Winter Ending

'A cold coming we had of it'
huddled together in cardboard cities,
crouched over shared books in leaking classrooms,
crammed into peeling waiting-rooms,
ice stamped into crazy-paving
round polluted streams.
Winter ending:
paintings, poems bud hesitantly,
tentative chords behind boarded façades;
factories open like daffodils,
trains flex frozen rheumatic joints,
computer-screens blink on
in the sudden daylight.
As the last cardboard boxes
are swept away beneath busy bridges,
the cold blue landscape of winter
suddenly alive with bright red roses.

The Grandmothers

We have silenced our grandmothers
MIES BOUWHUYS

We have silenced our grandmothers.
Rumpelstiltskin forgotten,
the spinning-wheel covered in dust.
Snow White's mirror is tarnished,
the words stuck in its throat.
Jack the Giant Killer's medals
are stuck at the back of a shelf
in a backstreet pawnshop.

The grandmothers are silent.
There is a house agent's sign
outside the Beast's castle;
the garden is choked with overgrown roses
that bloom no longer.
The doctors have decided
to switch off Sleeping Beauty's
life-support machine:
seven desolate dwarfs
wander the back lot of Universal Studios.

We have silenced our grandmothers.
The Princes, pale or otherwise,
have departed,
the Princesses having married
millionaire Texan playboys;
the last dragons are preserved
as endangered species
in distant game-parks:
the last grandmother unheard
above the neon blare
of TV screens.

Love Story, Bosnia
(i.m. Bosko Brokić and Admira Ismić)

Bosko and Admira
huddle near in no-man's-land,
hand almost touching hand.
They do not move as other lovers.

Dead cellars of Sarajevo.
Birds beat on the empty wind
Playground silence broken
by the cackle of assault rifles.

The sweater his mother knitted for her
lies on the grave her mother cannot visit.

Helpless as words,
their few flowers wilt in the indifferent sun.